Professional Partners Success Blueprint

A proven, step-by-step guide to developing profitable referrals from solicitors & accountants

Steve Billingham

GW00374465

stevebillingham.com

Contents

Acknowledgements

There are a number of people I'd like to thank for their help in getting this book "out there". The first is Kevin Ferriby (MD) and the team at Informed Financial Planning. It was IFP who originally gave me the idea of developing a step by step framework to help advisers develop referral relationships with solicitors and accountants, as part of the consultancy work I was undertaking with them.

Their input and feedback on the blueprint over the last 12 months has been pivotal in shaping and refining the end product. The fact that they adopted the blueprint as a core pillar of their strategy and have achieved such impressive results has proved that this blueprint works.

That made Kevin the natural choice to write the foreword to the book and I'm both delighted and grateful that he did. Thanks Kevin.

Next are Mark Ferris, of Entrust Financial Planners in Northwich and Paul Crawford of Crawford Consulting in Norwich, both of whom provided critical feedback about the blueprint content. Their feedback resulted in some fine-tuning and I genuinely appreciate their willingness to be critical, candid and constructive.

Next are the many firms who have been part of the Professional Partners Success Blueprint consultancy programme, a number of whom are responsible for the gushingly positive comments featured in the book. Thank you for participating and sharing your thoughts and reflections and for providing more evidence that "this stuff works".

I am so grateful to Nick Brown of Inspire for his thoughtful design and patience, as I asked for yet another tweak here or there and his speedy responses to my favourite question… "what would it look like if…? The man is a design genius.

I owe a huge debt of gratitude to Carrie Bendall, also of Inspire, who painstakingly proof read the first draft and offered the benefit of her experience as the "queen of communication" with suggested edits, additions and ideas and then even offered to write a guest chapter for the book. I'll miss my daily 8.30a.m. call with her latest suggestion.

Last but not least my biggest thank you is to my wife Sue, for her support and patience, both during the time it has taken to write the book (when I'm in "work mode" I can tend to become so focused that I tend not to see, hear or appreciate what is going on around me) and throughout the 30 years we have been married.

She is my rock, my best friend and keeps me grounded.

Feedback on "Professional Partners Success Blueprint"

The connection I made with a small Manchester accountant is progressing nicely with the first test cases commencing in the next few weeks. He decided he will ask his best client who has a £6m turnover business!

Whilst his firm is very creative and appears to offer a good service to clients, their processes are light years behind ours. The simple fact that I produced documents addressing his concerns, outlining the synergies and how we would shape our relationship in the future impressed him on their own.

When I also showed him examples of our meeting notes and reports it would be fair to say that he was very impressed.

As Financial Planners (particularly ones that have worked with a good business consultant like Steve) we need to appreciate just how far ahead we are of the other professions in terms of process and professionalism. I now have the confidence that if I can get in front of the right firms and follow the blueprint we have a good chance of success.

Mark Ferris, Entrust Financial Planning

The content of Professional Partners Success Blueprint is logical, inspirational and very easy to follow and digest. I would also heartily recommend Steve's consultancy programme to anyone who wants to become better at what they do. Thought provoking, yet reassuring in that we already have the ability and experience to break into this market and now, I believe, will have the benefit of support and direction from the learnings available from the blueprint. Thank you Steve!

Mark Cooper, Moneywise Financial Management

Thanks Steve, I found the Professional Partners Success Blueprint very useful. I'm now going to block some time out in my diary over the next 3 weeks to put together my action plan & DO IT! Hope to speak to you with some positive results.

Jim Cooper, Cooper & Associates Wealth Management

…very useful and thought provoking.

Lisa Johnstone, VWM Wealth

Found the Professional Partners Success Blueprint very informative and this has come at a great time for our business as we have made the decision to invest money & time into building a bank of introducers. This will kick start our campaign and provide the framework we need to be successful.

Plenty of good suggestions. Thanks for the inspiration.

Richard Houghton, Retirement Solutions (UK) Ltd

Thoroughly enjoyed the Professional Partners Success Blueprint. It was highly practical with lots of useful takeaways to help us get started working with professionals. Looking forward to beginning implementation of your ideas. This will help get over the biggest problem most of us have - namely taking the first step and gaining some momentum.

Martin Turbin, Turbin Wealth Management

… really useful and extremely informative.

Roger Milbourn, Financial Themes

Foreword

As a former Practising Accountant and currently Managing Director of one of the first firms of Chartered Financial Planners in the UK, I consider The Professional Partners Success Blueprint to be a worthy addition to the library of any Financial Planner looking to really make a success of developing valuable relationships with Professional Connections.

When I first entered the brave new world of Financial Services back in 1997 after a fifteen year stint in the Accountancy profession, the obvious way of attracting new clients was to forge alliances with the rest of the local professional community. Over the years, this met with some success although not as consistently as I would have liked and not in a way that was easily taught to colleagues as our business expanded.

The situation today is very different, largely as a result of working with the Author, Steve Billingham in recent years. Our business relationship started back in 2008 when we were looking to re-engineer our business in the run up the Retail Distribution Review resulting in the successful transition to a fee-based practice with improved client service at the core of what the business is about. As we worked with Steve, it became apparent that he could really add some value to our business by applying some of the same philosophies to our dealings with Professional Partners who provide us with the vast majority of our new clients. The success of these relationships is absolutely key to us achieving our strategic objectives.

We therefore worked with Steve on creating our Professional Partners Programme using the tools and techniques covered in this book. The results have been impressive, improving existing relationships and really helping in attracting new ones. We have designed service standards for our Professional Partners in the same way as we have for our clients and regularly add to our library of presentations on topics relevant to other professionals and their clients. Together with our programme of regular seminars and newsletter aimed specifically at Professional Partners this has helped to provide us with a stream of high quality clients and a standing in the local professional community that I am sure many other firms would relish.

I am absolutely convinced that if you are serious about achieving success with Professional Partners then your investment in time reading Steve's work will reap significant rewards.

Well done Steve on producing such a valuable piece of work for the Financial Planning community, I hope it will be the success you deserve it to be.

Kevin Ferriby, Chartered Financial Planner

Managing Director, Informed Financial Planning

Hull, June 2013

Introduction

I appreciate you making the commitment to take the time to read this book. The fact that you have done so tells me that you are serious about building a better business.

That is my sole aim. To help you do just that and I am confident that you will find it insightful and highly practical and that you'll feel that it has been time well spent.

This book is based on our successful "Professional Partners Success Blueprint", a consultancy programme which is aimed at advisers who are seeking to develop successful (defined as profitable, sustainable and long term) client referral relationships with solicitors and accountants. This Blueprint provides a unique framework designed specifically to help you to do that in a structured and professional way.

In this book I am going to share all my insights about what it takes to succeed in this market. The blueprint, which took over a year to design and create, has been built with input from firms who have already established successful introducer relationships with other professionals.

What does "successful" mean? How does over 100 referrals a year sound? That is what just one of the firms that I have worked with to develop this blueprint has consistently achieved. What would that level of success mean for your business?

This book will provide you with a step by step framework for doing the same.

At the centre of this framework lies the blueprint itself. The blueprint breaks down the relationship development process into 6 stages:

- Stage 1: Prepare
- Stage 2: Approach
- Stage 3: Initial meeting
- Stage 4: Nurture
- Stage 5: Implement
- Stage 6: Build & embed

This book will take you step by step through these 6 stages and identify the key objectives of each stage and the actions, activities, strategies and tactics you need to use to move through them in a way that builds your credibility, establishes trust and enhances your standing as a professional.

The book kicks off with why it makes sense to target solicitors and accountants for referrals and probably more importantly… why right now?

We then explore why you might have found it difficult in the past, or why you might not have achieved the results you were hoping for, despite maybe having spent a fair amount of time and effort to date, trying to do so.

Then we'll get into an overview of the blueprint itself and examine each of the six stages of the relationship development process in more detail.

Will reading the book guarantee success? Of course not. Only you can do that by applying the thinking and ideas contained throughout its pages.

What it will give you, is a proven success framework, lots of ideas, concepts, strategies and tactics, which when applied diligently and consistently, have the potential to transform your business results through professional referrals. At the end of the day, it's smart thinking and the doing that will make the difference, not the knowing.

01

Why Solicitors & Accountants & why now?

Well, primarily they frequently work with and very often can be the gatekeepers to attractive client niches. Niches such as:

- Businesses and their directors or partners and the senior personnel within those businesses
- People with complicated tax affairs
- High and Ultra High Net Worth individuals
- People who are themselves, or who are responsible for caring for personal injury or medical negligence claimants
- Widows and Divorcees
- Trustees
- Individuals, often the physically or mentally disabled and the elderly, and their families whose affairs are subject to lasting powers of attorney

Crucially, many of their clients can benefit significantly from the services that financial advisers and planners provide which makes them, potentially at least, a great source of good quality client referrals.

The better ones are actually receptive to referral relationships. By better, I mean the more client focused, the more entrepreneurial, the ones who look beyond just doing what's required and who are genuinely interested in helping their clients to achieve better outcomes through a more holistic and collaborative approach.

Relationships between financial advisers and solicitors and accountants, really should be a match made in heaven. Not too long ago, a fellow consultant (who specialises in working with accountants) and I, were lamenting the fact that in reality, these relationships seem harder to build than they should be.

He has accountant clients all over the UK who are really keen to find a local IFA who they can trust, to work with. I have IFA clients all over the UK who are keen to develop relationships with accountants. It really shouldn't be that hard… should it?

But why now?

The answer to the "why now?" question lies in the fact that many accountants and solicitors are facing a number of significant commercial challenges in their own businesses and practices right now. These challenges mean that they need to look for ways to build greater commercial resilience into their businesses.

And besides which, if you don't, somebody else will.

Challenges facing accountants

The findings that follow were published in a 2011 White Paper: "The biggest challenges facing the UK accountancy profession over the next 5 years." That White Paper was based on the responses of 108 accountants, each of whom was asked to identify their biggest concerns.

What stands out for me from this research is that the challenges that they face are very similar to the challenges IFAs have faced over recent years. Here's what they said.

1. Not enough of the right sort of clients

With the emphasis on right clients, not just more clients. In other words, profitable clients. The business valuation model for accountancy practices is based on a multiple of Gross Recurring Fees (GRF), (typically just 1 x GRF).

That leads accountants to focus on more clients (because by definition another client will increase GRF), not right clients. Replace GRF with Assets Under Management and the behaviour looks somewhat familiar to that of IFAs over recent years don't you think? "Asset gathering" has been the strategy rather than ensuring all clients are profitable.

2. Getting paid fees that reflect the quality of the work they do

Again a problem you will be familiar with, particularly in the post RDR world. Many accountants struggle to charge the level of fee that the work involved actually justifies. As a result, their recovery rate (the number of hours they can actually charge to the client v. the number of hours actually taken to do the work) is often lower than it should be.

They also suffer from what is known as "lock up" as a result of slow paying clients, work in progress, high debtor days and bad debts. One accountant told me at a recent seminar, that they deliberately quote a price that they think will win them the business and if the work turns out to be more complex, invoice the client for a higher fee than the original quote.

In other words, they know that there are always difficult fee conversations to be had with clients. So they have clearly got their pricing challenges too. Far better, don't you think, to invoice the client for less than you originally quoted?

3. External threats

They are facing a number of external threats, such as:

- Home based accountants, many of whom are unqualified, offering low cost core compliance services such as company incorporations or preparation of self-employed tax returns.

- The introduction of technology that makes it cheaper and easier to carry out commoditised "compliance" work.
- Poor service from HMRC, which is creating additional work, slowing things down and putting pressure on cash flow.

4. Getting new clients

Accountants don't really understand marketing and certainly don't like "selling". They are also often reluctant to bring in people with the right skills, profile and experience to take on these functions, or to outsource them to a third party.

The fact is, most accountants have had no formal sales or marketing training. Their training has been focused on getting qualified, which by definition means focusing on the technical aspects. They've been trained to think that "technical excellence" is all that matters. Sure, it's important, but on its own, it won't guarantee a successful practice.

Like you, they are also really busy people, focused on delivering great value and great service (hopefully) for their clients. So, they struggle to find the time to focus on "business development".

5. Finding, keeping and motivating the right team

Many accountants are worried that they don't have the right people in the business to take over the practice (sound familiar?). They are concerned about sub-standard work impacting quality and service levels and consequently they are sometimes reluctant to delegate to people who are perfectly capable of doing the job well.

They are also not immune from staff turnover and can face high recruitment costs due to high staff attrition.

6. Other challenges

They are also facing a number of other impacts on productivity, which may not, on the face of it at least, be so "business critical", but nevertheless, they do ultimately impact their profitability, service and results. These include:

- Time and workload management (due to poor delegation, doing the wrong work, poor client quality or just poor time management, personal productivity and effectiveness).
- Pricing pressures (as a result of not enough chargeable hours being recorded and billed by fee earners, which leads to poor cashflow and pressure on margins).
- Lack of business skills. (I don't mean that in a critical way. It's just they are technicians. They've been told throughout their training and whilst they were

working their way up to full partner, that technical excellence was all they needed, to be successful. They haven't had or invested in leadership training, people management skills or sales and marketing skills).

Challenges facing solicitors

Now you won't be surprised to hear that solicitors face many of the same problems as accountants.

1. Getting new clients

Like accountants, except maybe even more so, solicitors don't understand marketing and don't like "selling". Their relationships with clients are usually transactional, so by definition, they are reliant on finding new clients all the time. Very often, using a solicitor is a distress purchase. You only go to one when there's a specific problem.

Their language reflects this transaction focus. They talk about "matters" not people. And again they haven't usually had much or any formal sales and marketing training.

Getting paid fees that reflect the quality of the work they do is a problem for solicitors too.

2. Silo structure or mentality

Solicitors often work in silos or have a silo mentality because, very often, a firm of solicitors is no more than a group of individuals working as a "co-operative" under the same roof. Consequently, there can be a significant degree of disinterest in business or practice management issues. No brand value is being created and very often there is little or no cross referral. In fact one of our clients told me recently that one of her solicitor connections had said that her department (which handled matrimonial issues) and the probate department rarely spoke to each other. I find that staggering.

3. External threats

Solicitors are also facing some significant external threats. I'm sure you're all aware of the Legal Services Act which introduced increased competition from low cost suppliers. But for many, the Jackson Reforms and changes to the funding of legal aid are causing big problems and potential future revenue holes and margin squeeze for firms.

These threats are significant, very real and are having a massive impact on legal firms right now, today.

Here's what SIFA had to say about it in one of their recent newsletters…

Alarm in the solicitor market

"It has for long been anticipated that the number of law firms would decline in the face of the competition created by the Legal Services Act. However, the immediate problems facing the profession are the result not of the Act but of civil justice reform and changes to the legal aid system, combined with difficulty in obtaining funding, partners distributing rather than retaining profits and, in some cases, taking on expensive property commitments. Five prominent UK firms have folded over recent months. The Solicitors Regulation Authority intervened in 30 firms in 2012 and it is currently discussing possible intervention in a further 56 firms to protect clients' interests. The Law Society has taken "emergency steps" which include setting up a dedicated web site to help solicitors "worried about the viability of their firms".

A major underlying issue is the fact that many solicitors are operating an out-dated and broken business model which centres on transactional business and lacks the client databases which might assist them to maintain on-going client relationships. Also, the failed Quality Solicitors experiment with W H Smith underlines the fact that that many consumers regard legal services as a necessary evil, associated with the negatives in life, such as death, divorce, litigation and moving house. And very few firms are thinking outside the legal box by taking positive step to enhance their business proposition by diversifying their client offering beyond legal services. The lead in this respect is coming from the newcomers to the legal market, such as the Co-Op, AA and Saga, who regard legal services as an adjunct to their existing client proposition and a means of maximising cross-selling opportunities.

Financial advisers who share solicitors' ethical principles are uniquely well positioned to assist solicitors in this situation. Financial issues pervade many areas of legal work and the combination of legal and financial services provides the basis for the crucial trusted adviser role which is key to client retention. An obvious area of potential collaboration is the sharing of IFAs' factfind data on referred clients."

Source: Ian Muirhead, SIFA Newsletter, April 2013

4. Technology

Technology that makes it cheaper and easier to carry out commoditised "compliance" work is a factor, but in the case of solicitors it's services like will writing or conveyancing that are coming under pressure.

And of course, because solicitors are running businesses, they face many of the same challenges we saw for accountants around time management, finding, keeping and motivating the right team, poor cashflow and lock up and lack of business and marketing skills.

A specific and very common technology shortcoming for solicitors is a distinct lack of client data and effective databases, which makes relationship building and marketing difficult to say the least.

In other words, there has never been a better time to try to establish relationships with solicitors and accountants. What are you waiting for?

02

What's the problem?

So, why do financial advisers find developing these relationships challenging? It comes back largely to what they say and do or, to be more accurate, what they don't say and what they don't do!

1. Reputational Risk

If you start by thinking about the issue of referring clients from the solicitor's or accountant's perspective, what perceptions or concerns are they likely to have? Let's be honest, justified or not, the IFA sector doesn't enjoy the best of reputations.

The consultant who specialises in working with accountants, who I mentioned in Chapter 1, said that the main reason accountants are fearful of referring their clients to an IFA is that, in their experience, they don't do what they say they are going to do. He told me that one of his clients is currently working with an IFA that they have big concerns about, because he "doesn't do what he says he is going to do". They are actively looking for a new adviser relationship for that reason.

Yes, the IFA sector is changing with higher qualifications, increased professionalism, more transparency and greater regulation but the fact remains that their biggest fear in introducing their clients to you, is reputational risk and fear over the quality of your advice. You might not like it. You might say that it isn't justified or fair, but they're the facts. Only you can change their perceptions.

The fact is that, in referring their clients to a third party, solicitors and accountants are putting their reputation and relationship with the client, on the line. They are going to be cautious. You would be too in their position.

2. Poor targeting

Advisers in my experience don't spend enough (or even any) time identifying the characteristics of the firms they want to work with or thinking about the criteria they will use to prioritise which firms to approach first, such as size of firm relative to the IFA practice, age of partners, geography or key areas of specialism.

3. No structure, strategy or objectives

The approach to building relationships is usually unstructured and little time is spent considering:

- What specific objectives do we want to achieve?
- What specific steps and materials might be needed to support the relationship development process?
- What specific actions and tactics are needed to move the relationship to the next stage?
- How to build credibility and trust a step at a time?

A lack of clarity and answers to these questions, can lead to a perception of a lack of professionalism.

4. No nurturing

Advisers often fail to invest enough time to educate solicitors and accountants, or fail to nurture the relationship through regular contact, identifying opportunities, providing education, resources, support and value along the way.

5. Poor (or non-existent) follow up

Another failing can be poor or inconsistent follow up after any initial meeting. This is just a lack of process or discipline. It's about following a clear process to thank them for their time, to confirm what's been agreed and diarising the next contact. Find reasons to keep in touch.

6. Lack of patience and persistence

Advisers also give up too quickly when referrals aren't produced in the first month. They tend to give in and move on, get back on the hamster wheel and overlook the need to nurture the relationship and the need to stay connected, keep communicating and to keep building their credibility and profile. This is a slow burn.

Advisers who are successful in building relationships have often devoted many years to the cause. Don't be disheartened though. One adviser I have worked with saw immediate and significant success (£30,000 in revenue in just 7 months) using the principles in this book. Others have enjoyed immediate success in terms of both securing initial meetings and early referrals.

7. Unrealistic expectations

It's important not to expect results too quickly. You have to take the relationship through the know/ like/trust phases before you can expect even a sniff of a referral (think back to the earlier point about the potential for reputational damage and putting the client relationship on the line).

Would you refer your clients to a solicitor or accountant after just one or even two meetings with no evidence about the quality of their work and service? No, nor would I. That would be madness, bordering on negligence. It's about building rapport, empathy, trust and credibility quickly but professionally.

The Professional Partners Success Blueprint provides the framework to help you do that.

03

The Success Blueprint – an overview

Here's the approach we've taken to creating the Professional Partner Success Blueprint. We've broken the relationship development process down into a six stage framework and identified the tools, tactics, content and marketing collateral that will help you to build your credibility and demonstrate your professionalism from day 1.

Stage 1: Prepare

Stage 1 is essentially about getting your house in order in terms of your core marketing and support materials (including your website) and carrying out your initial research and preparation about which firms to target and why? The starting point should be to clearly define the objectives you are looking to achieve, whether that is a specific level of revenue, profit or number of referrals. You then need to establish clarity about which firms you want to target and what criteria you intend to use to make those decisions.

Stage 2: Approach

Here's where you start to map out how to approach and connect with the firms you've identified. You need to think about what type of approach is likely to be most effective for the firms you've targeted.

The interesting thing here is that, according to the research 40% of accountants and solicitors questioned said that they had relationships with advisers who had approached them, rather than the other way around.

In other words they tend to be passive, which means you'll have to make the first move typically. If you are waiting for them to come to you, you may need lots of patience.

Stage 3: Initial meeting

The initial meeting is your one and only chance to make a good first impression. How are you going to evidence your credibility and start to build trust from the outset?

How can you make sure that you establish rapport, ask the right questions and build your credibility a step at a time? How do you position you and your firm effectively from the off?

Stage 4: Nurturing

Nurturing the relationship is critical. How can you make sure that you follow up consistently and effectively and develop the relationship over time?

This stage is about creating a robust process for following up and keeping the dialogue and relationship moving forwards. Very few professionals will refer clients on the back of one meeting.

Nurturing looks at what you need to be doing after the initial meeting. It's crucial to take an approach that is both professional and structured. One that takes the relationship forward a step at a time.

Stage 5: Implementation

Implementation is the point at which you reach agreement to enter into a referral relationship. It's also about cementing the relationship and establishing a formal introducer agreement and celebrating the fact that you have agreed to work together.

Stage 6: Build and embed

The final stage is where you capitalise on all the good work to this point by developing a formal marketing plan, establishing a clear referral process, and explore ways in which you can bring financial planning services to the attention of their clients through a client communication plan.

Build and embed also includes establishing a contact plan for keeping in touch with the centres of influence and referral within each firm, identifying joint marketing opportunities and implementing an appropriate set of metrics to track the result.

04

Stage 1: Prepare

Preparation is everything and there are a number of things that I believe you need to have in place, before you start trying to "connect" with any potential partner firms.

Most firms don't need many successful referral relationships to achieve their revenue and new client acquisition targets, but how do you decide which firms to target?

The place to start is by clearly defining your objectives. For example:

- What are you are trying to achieve?
- How many new clients are you looking for?
- What level of revenue/recurring income/profit are you looking to generate?
- How many referrals will you need each week or month to generate the required number of clients? (What is your enquiry to client conversion rate?)
- How many new referrals can you handle effectively, without overloading the back office or affecting the service delivered to your existing clients?

Once you're clear about your objectives, you can start to look at which firms to target.

Which firms should we target?

Identifying a sensible set of criteria, against which you can rank each potential target firm for suitability, will increase the chances of establishing successful, profitable, long-term relationships. Here are some criteria that it makes sense to use.

Geography

Presumably, you will want to restrict your efforts to your local area (maybe regional) to keep things sensible from a travel perspective. Not only do you want to be able to manage the relationship through regular face to face contact, you also need to make sure that you can fulfil any referrals you get without travelling the length and breadth of the UK. Local firms will be working (in the main at least) with local clients.

Size

If you run a small, single adviser practice, you are unlikely to be seen as having sufficient scale by PWC. It may be better to target firms of a similar size to your own practice, to avoid concerns over your ability to fulfil.

This isn't a hard and fast rule. Small professional practices may feel that a bigger advisory firm gives them a greater degree of security. Conversely, larger firms may feel happier knowing that they are dealing with the owner of the advisory business.

In general though, my advice would be to look for firms with a similar number of partners and fee earners to your own business.

Age of the partners

Are they of an age that suggests they are in it for the long term, or are they just crossing off the days to retirement? Are they of a similar age to you? You are more likely to relate and "connect" with people with similar ambition to you.

Areas of specialisms

Is there a good fit between their specialisms and your specific areas of expertise or ideal client profile? For example, when targeting solicitors, the following legal specialisms all offer significant financial planning opportunities;

- Trust and estate work
- Older clients
- Family law
- Court of Protection and personal injury trusts
- Corporate
- Trustee work
- Offshore and expat work

Reputation

What is their local profile and reputation like? What do you, your staff, your clients, know about them? Are they well established and highly regarded?

Professional listings

Check them out on the Institute of Chartered Accountants for England and Wales (ICAEW), Association of Chartered Certified Accountants (ACCA) or Law Society website. What does it tell you about them? How long have they been established? These listings will also help you to establish the age, names and number of partners.

Their website

What does it say about the services they provide, the type of clients they work with and their people? Are there lots of great testimonials from delighted clients that suggest that they would be a great firm for you to refer your clients to. Would you add them to your own shortlist of "possibles" if you were in need of the services they offer?

Does it send the right message about the quality of the firm? Do they do client events (great opportunity for joint marketing initiatives)? Do they have lots of useful information and educational content on their website that is engaging to clients?

Social media

Look them up on LinkedIn. What groups do they belong to? Are they active? If so, it is evidence that they are taking "business development" seriously, which means they are more likely to be open to exploring opportunities to work with third parties to do so?

Don't be tempted to try to shortcut this research stage. It will save you a lot of fruitless meetings, give you lots of knowledge and lots to talk about.

Positioning you and your services effectively

Ok, so we've done our initial research. What do we need to do to prepare? To make sure we position ourselves effectively.

Here, I want to look at 4 key things you need to think about:

- Key attributes
- 60 second pitch
- Your website and what it says about you
- What collateral materials will you need to look credible, serious and professional?

Key attributes

In late 2009 JP Morgan Asset Management published a research paper that, amongst other things, looked at the attributes that solicitors and accountants look for in any advisory firm they might choose to work with. That paper was titled "Professional Connections: Creating opportunities between IFAs and other advisory professionals" and is freely available on the JP Morgan Asset Management website at …

http://am.jpmorgan.co.uk/adviser/adviserresearchandreports/professionalconnections/

The most important criteria are, in no particular order and perhaps unsurprisingly:

1. Qualifications

Solicitors & accountants are obviously well qualified and will expect financial planners and advisers to be well qualified too.

2. Local profile and reputation

Most solicitors and accountants are looking for a firm with an excellent local profile and reputation, so glowing testimonials, compelling case studies and positive media exposure or community involvement can all help in this area.

Some advisers for example play an active role in the local business community through things like the local Chamber of Trade or Chamber of Commerce or by getting involved and supporting local charities.

The key thing for me is to get involved in these groups for the right reason. Don't just join to make up the numbers. Play an active role. Join to make a difference and follow your passion. That way you can build your credibility and your reputation.

3. Clear proposition and expertise

Solicitors and accountants are also looking for firms with a clear proposition and area of expertise.

Solicitors in particular tend to specialise. They can therefore be a bit sceptical about advisers who claim to be experts in all areas. So emphasise any specialisms you have, particularly where they are relevant to the high value areas of advice such as maybe Trustee Investment, Pension Sharing, IHT Mitigation or Tax Planning.

4. Fee based advice model, not commission based sales model.

There is a clear preference for a fee based model. They prefer a business model focused on the delivery of advice and are highly sceptical about businesses focused on product sales.

5. Experience

Experience is relevant but less important. In fact according to the J P Morgan data, about half as relevant.

6. Cultural and Personal Fit

Needless to say, if they are referring clients they are looking for a good cultural and personal fit and of course they'll be interested in the extent to which you might be able to refer business to them. Don't overpromise. Be realistic, honest and manage expectations appropriately.

Interestingly, one word not on this list of key criteria is "size". Size appears not to be important, which reaffirms what I said earlier about size not being a hard and fast issue. However, beware the scalability and fulfilment concerns I mentioned – bigger firms in particular, may have concerns about your ability to fulfil client referrals effectively, if they perceive that everything in the business depends on you.

Another word missing from the list is "money" or "pay away". Now I'm not suggesting that solicitors & accountants aren't interested in the commercial side of the relationship, but this research suggests that it's not a top priority. Indeed there are regulatory restrictions in place regarding how and even whether they can receive financial reward from the work of third parties. So leading with the "financials" discussion, is unlikely to be the best tactic.

Remember, they will be looking for evidence in respect of all these areas. They won't just take your word for it.

We'll be revisiting this list of criteria later, when we'll dive a lot deeper into these key issues and explore how you can evidence your credentials against each.

60 second pitch

Your 60 second pitch is simply a 1 minute summary of what you do, who for and how those people feel when you've done it. You can and should use this at networking and other events or in answer to the question... what do you do?

Here's a suggested format that you can try to follow when you are creating your version.

I work with...

Be specific about who you work with, e.g. business owners/divorcees/trustees/retail executives.

You might also include characteristics such as age, occupation, life stage or geography.

Who have problems with...

Describe the specific challenge or problem that your typical clients are trying to solve (their "pain").

What I do is...

Explain what you do to solve the problem. Use clear simple language that both a 13 and 85 year old could understand. It is not about proving how clever you are.

So that...

Give a simple explanation of the solution that the client gets.

Which means...

List the benefits in a compelling way that connects both rationally and emotionally with the client.

Example – 60 second pitch

Here's an example containing each of the key elements...

"I work with widows and divorcees... who are struggling with managing their finances now that their husband or partner is no longer around to take care of things.

I help them to understand their current financial position and put in place a plan to manage their money effectively and even tell them how much they can afford to spend... so that they feel more in control of their financial situation... which means they can live their life, without worrying about every penny".

A tad more engaging than "I'm a financial adviser" don't you think?

The Acid Test

Once you've created your 60 second pitch, ask yourself these 4 questions:

1. Does it sound compelling, interesting and do you come across as passionate and authentic?

2. Will the listener clearly understand what your business does?

3. Does it roll off the tongue easily and smoothly?

4. Does it pass the 13 and 85 year-old test?

Now, what about your website?

Your website will be the first place that any prospective referral partner is going to go to check you out, possibly followed by your LinkedIn profile.

Whatever method of contact you adopt (more on that in the next chapter), the minute contact is made, they are likely to check out your website, so now is the time to make sure it won't let you down when they do so.

The characteristics of a really good website are beyond the scope of this book, but here are a few searching questions to get you thinking:

- Are you visible and easily found?
- Does your website look professional?
- Does it differentiate you and show your business in the best light, or is it just like every other financial adviser's website (full of techno-babble and me/we content)?
- Does it make them stop and take notice because it stands out from a design perspective?
- Does it have lots of content and evidence that reinforces your position as an expert in your field?
- Are there lots of highly visible testimonials and case studies that showcase your best work and what your clients think about you?
- Does it help them to see that you really understand the problems that your (and their) target market is facing, or does it just bang on about you and your services?

- Does it make them feel as though they have come to the right place?
- When was it last updated?

If you really want to get serious or use professional referrals as your main new client acquisition strategy, you may want to consider setting up a dedicated area for solicitors and accountants (one for each) on your website to provide, for example:

- Financial services news and updates
- Legal/Accountancy news and updates
- Tax and technical updates
- Client referral forms

Collateral Materials

Once you put yourself "out there" and try to connect with accountants and solicitors, the danger is that one or two of them agree to meet with you for an exploratory meeting.

In order to look professional, make the right impression and look like a proper business, you'll need to have some tangible marketing materials to back you up. These materials don't need to cost the earth, but they do need to look and feel professional.

The preparation stage is the time to consider what materials you'll need. The simplest way is to create a selection of compelling, well designed materials to leave with those professionals with whom you do have initial meetings.

But what should you put in it?

Here's a list of the possible items/content you might want to consider including. I'm not suggesting you need all of this on day 1 before you start trying to connect with potential introducers. Some can be developed and added over time, but the first 5/6 items are probably the minimum you'll need to start with.

About us:

A document that summarises the firms history, values, services, ideal clients and approach. It's critical that the things that you say about your business in these materials is consistent with what you say on your website.

Client proposition:

An outline of the range of services that each client segment receives.

Staff biographies or team profile:

A document containing the brief biography, photo, title, experience, qualifications and contact information for each principal, advisor and key employee of the business. You might choose to do one for each principal and adviser and one covering the rest of the team, or keep things simple by just having one document which profiles the whole team.

A first meeting presentation:

A copy of your professional partners first meeting presentation slides. This presentation should simply tell the story about who you are, what you do, who you do it for and how you do it. If there are more than 10 slides, it's too long!

Case studies:

Single sheet items that showcase your best work. They should be relevant to your target market and provide background on the client, the challenges and issues they faced, what you did and the results achieved.

Testimonials:

A selection of genuine and compelling testimonials from delighted clients (satisfied doesn't cut it). What you are looking for is life changing remarks, to demonstrate the impact you have had on the lives of the clients you work with.

Ideal client profiles:

Details of your "ideal clients", describing the types of client you are best able to help.

Advice process:

Your advice or client engagement process, in diagramatic form if possible.

Relationship management overview:

A description of how the relationship between you and your professional introducers will work with regard to ongoing contact, communication and progress updates.

And of course a printed and branded "pocket type" folder to put it all in!

End of Stage 1: Preparation Checklist

1. Review your website: does it send the right message?

2. Start your research: identify which firms seem to make the right targets to approach. Look for alignment between their specialisms and your expertise. Look at their website and check out the individual partners. Find out more about each person via the ICAEW, ACCA or Law Society website and by checking their LinkedIn profile if they've got one.

3. Conduct an honest appraisal about how your business stacks up against the selection criteria we identified in this chapter.

4. Put together your 60 second pitch: does it satisfy the acid test?

5. Consider what collateral materials you want to include in your information pack. Differentiate between items you want available on day 1 and items you want to develop over time. You may already have some of the required items in your current suite of marketing materials. Start to put these materials together.

05

Stage 2: The Approach

In this chapter I want to explore the most effective strategies to connect and give you some specific ideas on how to make contact.

I cannot over-emphasise the importance of being crystal clear about the objective of each stage of the relationship development process. That's why advisers often have lots of meetings that don't go anywhere; they haven't got a clearly defined outcome or objective that they want to achieve from that specific meeting.

Set a clear objective

So, what is the objective of stage 2: "The approach"

Whichever connection strategy you adopt, the single objective is to get their agreement to meet for an hour or so. That's it. This is about moving one step at a time.

In that meeting your goal should be to:

- Find out more about them and their practice
- Explain who you are and what you do
- Establish whether it makes sense to explore in more detail how you might work together
- Either way… agree clear next steps

Anything more than that is delusional.

7 ways to connect

There are many ways in which you might make your initial approach and different approaches will work more or less effectively for different firms. I've tried to identify below, potential ways for you to try to connect with other professionals in the order of most to least effective. Whilst we could spend hours debating whether or not speaking is more effective than networking, in reality, the answer will depend on the size of your particular business and your personal strengths and level of confidence.

1. Mutual client introduction

This really is the number one way to connect with other professionals. It's a no brainer, so easy and so effective. Asking your existing clients to introduce you to their accountant or solicitor is all it takes.

Suggesting to your clients, particularly those of higher net worth, that their accountant or solicitor should probably be involved in a meeting where you will be making recommendations, is probably the single most effective way to connect.

IFA clients who have used this approach, have quickly been able to establish a high level of credibility and demonstrate their client centric approach.

This approach also provides you with the ideal opportunity to briefly explain what you do and show them how you do it.

The result should be more referrals of the professional's other clients. Why wouldn't their clients want more joined up thinking?

This strategy works particularly well with accountants in our experience. Even if you can't get a personal introduction, if you know who your client's solicitors or accountants are, you can always reach out to them using the mutual client to establish a connection and some common ground.

2. Your existing clients' needs

An approach that uses the fact that your existing clients occasionally ask you to recommend a solicitor/accountant and that you would like to discuss their services and areas of specialisation is unlikely to get rejected. Just like you, they are running a business. They need new clients too. Remember, "finding new clients" is also one of their biggest challenges too.

Be careful not to create an unrealistic level of expectation about how often this happens, as you don't want to blow your credibility. If you use this approach you need to be able to back it up with the occasional referral. But we know that a carefully crafted letter or email along these lines will, more often than not, receive a positive reception. We've seen success rates of 80% from some of our tailored initial approach letters and emails.

It's important though, to keep control by promising to call them in a few days time, to see whether they feel that an hour's meeting is worth their while. Doing so significantly increases your approach letter to initial meeting conversion rate.

3. Networking

Not everyone enjoys networking but most networking groups are likely to have solicitors and accountants attending. I attended the monthly marketing meeting of one of our accountancy clients recently and they had a whole agenda item on the networking activity that had been undertaken during the month and the new client opportunities that had resulted. Accountants in particular, take networking seriously.

If you can identify where other professionals hang out with their peers, in numbers, you're increasing your chances of success. Just like IFAs, solicitors and accountants have local and regional professional or CPD gatherings. The ICAEW website, for example, has a list of the various regions, the events that are taking place and the name and contact details of the regional co-ordinator.

The key thing to remember about networking is that the most important part of the process is effective follow up. If you aren't going to follow up systematically, don't waste your time going in the first place.

Networking is a skill and at the end of this book you will find a bonus chapter on how to network effectively, written by Carrie Bendall of Inspire, a business development and marketing consultancy that we have worked with for a number of years.

4. Running seminars and webinars

This is an approach that one adviser I'm currently working with has used regularly and successfully. They usually have a great response from their professional contacts. They pick relevant topics, occasionally use external speakers (including me from time to time) and will get 10 to 20 professionals to their office on a quarterly basis. They also do a regular newsletter specifically for their list of professional connections, which is a great way to keep "front of mind" and build their credibility and profile as trusted experts.

This firm really is now seen as "THE" firm of advisers by local introducers. Webinars are also a great way to engage an audience. They are easy to do, very low cost (no venue costs and the technology required starts from as little as £24pm) and just as effective as live events for establishing your credentials.

So if you have a list (or can put one together) of solicitors or accountants, inviting them to a free short breakfast or lunchtime webinar is a great way to raise your profile. But the topic has to be relevant, stimulating and engaging to their market. The range of potential topics is massive and this approach gives you the opportunity to create a series of webinars that individuals are likely to tune into regularly, thereby building your reputation, profile and credibility further over time.

5. Attending and speaking at their events

The quickest way to establish your credibility, professionalism and generate interest and awareness is through public speaking. Again not everyone's cup of tea or strength, but the skills can be learned and the fear, overcome.

The potential financial planning opportunities related to the work that solicitors and accountants do are extensive and all can make great topics for relevant presentations.

The professional gatherings and events I talked about above are a tremendous opportunity for you to offer your speaking services for free (in return for the contact details of the attendees preferably) on a topic relevant to the audience.

6. Social Media

I have what I like to think is a healthy level of scepticism about the value of social media for attracting new clients. When someone says to you "you have got to be on twitter" or "you have to have a Facebook page" your first question ought to be… "Why?"

Twitter and LinkedIn make sense for me because my target market hang out there in large numbers. It could make sense for you, if your target market does too. Otherwise, it can be a huge distraction from the far more effective strategy of getting off your backside and going to meet with a few people.

Having said all that, LinkedIn seems to be the social media platform of choice for most professionals. There are loads of LinkedIn "Groups" aimed at solicitors, accountants and their specific areas of specialism.

Some are national, some are more local, some are specialist, but spending a bit of time researching which groups are out there and joining those that seem to be the best fit in terms of connecting with your target audience will be time well spent.

Once you have joined a group, it's important to be active by:

- Watching and learning, initially at least
- Contributing to discussions that are posted
- Starting your own discussions on relevant topics once you've found your feet
- Connecting with individual group members directly, particularly those who are local
- Posting discussions about any seminars or webinars you've got planned
- Inviting specific individuals to attend
- Linking your blog posts automatically to your LinkedIn profile
- Drawing attention to any relevant material you read or write
- Seeking to connect "face to face" once the "virtual" relationship is strong enough
- If you're into social media, you could even start a "local professionals" group of your own.

7. Write to them or pick up the phone

A carefully crafted letter can be a very effective way to connect, particularly if the content is related to a mutual client or your existing client needs. However, a speculative phone call is unlikely to get the 80% success rate that a mutual client or potential referral discussion can get.

What are you going to do?

So, what are the best ways to actually make contact to try to get their agreement to meet for an hour? Remember that's the objective we set out to achieve.

You might write to them, send them an email or even call them using the mutual client approach or your ability to potentially refer clients to them when the need arises. Or even both. For a "cold" approach, a letter is probably going to appear more professional than an email.

One of our clients tried this approach recently and sent out just 5 letters to local solicitors. Those 5 letters resulted in 4 meetings, one of whom was so keen to meet up, that he offered to come to the adviser's office.

If you've met them at a networking event, maybe you can afford to be less formal and use email or the phone to follow up. If you're calling be prepared, positive and passionate.

Use your" 60 second pitch" to briefly explain who you are, who you work with and what you do. You'll remember in the previous chapter, we gave you a tool to help you create your 60 second pitch. Use it!

Get the commitment to meet for an hour or, if they just aren't the right person to talk to, get the name of the best individual to contact to have that meeting. Are they likely to say no when you've told them that you've got clients who, from time to time, might need their help?

When they agree to meet with you send them an appointment confirmation by email or letter to confirm the date timing and venue for the meeting and maybe a suggested agenda to make sure you both get real commercial value from the meeting, rather than it just being a cosy or informal chat that doesn't really go anywhere.

End of Stage 2: Approach Checklist

Here are your actions for implementation for Stage 2.

1. Decide on the most effective connection strategies for you and your business.

2. Create a compelling "mutual client" or "existing client needs" approach letter and email.

3. Identify local or regional networking groups and try out those that look most promising.

4. Establish whether any local Law Society or ICAEW groups meet regularly in your part of the UK and if so, reach out to the regional co-ordinator or chairperson.

5. Check out the websites of your "target firms" to find open events run by them, for their target market. If you find any, pitch up and put your networking skills to work.

06

Stage 3: The Initial Meeting

Ok, so you managed to get them to agree to an initial meeting. What happens when you get there? In this chapter I am going to give you some ideas and strategies for establishing rapport, building credibility and gaining trust during the first meeting. We will also look at the common mistakes to avoid.

What's the objective?

I won't make any apology for being obsessive compulsive about setting objectives. It's important to be absolutely clear what your objective is at each stage of the relationship development process. That objective will depend on the size of your firm and the firm in question.

For sure, you will want to establish rapport and build some initial credibility.

You'll want to find out a lot more about them and give them a better understanding of who you are, what you do, and how you do it.

And of course, you will want to make an assessment of the potential for developing a profitable relationship with the firm based on their ability to refer enough clients of the right quality on a regular basis.

But fundamentally your objective should be to reach agreement to keep the relationship moving forward… or not.

And that may simply be a further meeting with, perhaps, all the partners present to talk in more detail about how you believe you can help them create great outcomes for their clients. Or if it's a very small firm, it might be a second meeting to walk through some of the key financial planning opportunities as they relate to their specific areas of specialism.

Know your audience

The first thing I should say about this first meeting is to ensure that you know exactly who you are meeting with so that you can assess their likely level of authority.

Are they a genuine decision maker or are they likely to simply be a stepping-stone to reach the key decision makers?

Secondly, consider the location of the meeting. Do you want to meet at their office, on their turf or would it be better to meet off site somewhere, over coffee for example?

Repeat or reaffirm the purpose and possible outcomes for the meeting.

Once you get to the meeting itself, it's really helpful, as well as looking professional, to confirm the purpose and possible outcomes of the meeting. You'll remember that when you secured the appointment in stage 1 of the process you sent a confirmation email with a suggested agenda. Now is the time to just make sure that this suggested agenda will cover everything they want to cover as well.

So for example you might say something like…

"As I said in my email, the purpose of the meeting is to discuss your business, the services you provide, the types of client you work with and see whether any of the services we each provide can help us to make a real difference to our respective key clients. I'll obviously provide an overview of who we are, what we do and answer any questions you have about me, our business, or our services. Is there anything specific you would like to make sure we cover during the meeting?"

If they come up with anything add it to the agenda.

You might then go on to say… "At the end of the meeting, one of two outcomes is likely. We might feel that there just isn't a good fit between what we do and how you work with your clients and that it doesn't make sense to progress things. If that's the case, it's not a problem. That's just business, we're never going to be right for everyone and I don't want you to feel awkward about saying that, if that's how you feel."

"Alternatively, we may feel that there's a really good fit and that it makes sense to take things to the next stage which is normally to schedule another meeting, involving your other partners and key personnel to explain more specifically how we think we can work together. Does that make sense?"

Now to some people, suggesting that we may choose not to work together is counter intuitive. Why say that? Because it's true! This is about being seen to be professional, about building credibility and about building trust. It's also about being seen to be different.

I'd suggest that it is very unlikely anyone has said that to them before. You've just gone a long way to achieving those things by being open, honest, and acknowledging their right to say "no". And you've taken the pressure off them. It's changed from being a pitch, to being a two-way discussion.

Be curious

It's really important to adopt a fact finding mentality and to start with the goals and objectives of their business before going into "about us" mode. David Sandler, founder of The Sandler Institute, a US based sales training business, had a saying that goes...

"You establish your credibility by the questions you ask, not by the information you give".

Credibility is what we want here, so ask great questions. Questions like:

- What are the long term objectives and goals of the practice?

- What do you believe makes you different to your peers and competitors?
- Do you have any current formal referral relationships with other professional firms?
- In what way do your referral partners contribute to the strategic development of your practice?
- How do you feel about your practice referring clients for financial services and investment advice?
- What concerns do you have about referring your clients to a professional financial planning firm?

Discuss some of the key challenges they are facing as a business. We looked at these in Chapter 1. Research the background to the big issues, so that you appear informed and credible.

With a solicitor for example, you might talk to them about the Legal Services Act, or the Jackson reforms or the changes to legal aid funding and the impact these changes are having on their practice. Remember Scotland is different!

Establish whether the practice is a genuine business or more of a "co-operative" of disparate individuals. Many are, particularly solicitors, but also some accountancy practices where each of the partners does their thing, their way. If it is more of a co-operative this means that you might have to get the buy in of each decision maker one at a time in respect of referring their clients, rather than developing a practice wide relationship from outset.

Then you can talk about you! Communicate your key "about us" messages in a compelling way. Use a simple deck of about a dozen PowerPoint or Keynote slides to explain who you are, what you do and why you're different.

Follow up is critical

Follow up after the meeting thanking them for their time, summarising the agreed actions/ commitments and timescales and enclosing your "Information Pack". Alternatively, leave the pack with them at the end of the meeting, but still follow up thanking them for their time and summarising the agreed next steps.

Addressing their concerns

Now, it's critical that you understand the key concerns and criteria that solicitors and accountants consider when selecting a partner to work with.

You also need to understand any existing relationships and the decision making process for changing that. If there is a really solid relationship in place, it may make sense to cut your losses and move on. However, a great question where that is the case is… "If there's one thing that your current partner could do better, what would it be? It might identify a weak link and leave the door open.

Satisfying their selection criteria

Earlier, we looked at the key attributes accountants and solicitors are looking for. We also established that they will be looking for real tangible proof that you meet those criteria. How can you evidence and demonstrate your credentials in each of these areas and address the key concerns that they have about referring their clients to you?

Below we offer a reminder of some of the key selection criteria together with some of the key concerns that you will need to address in order to move the relationship through the KNOW, LIKE, TRUST stages of the relationship. Under each heading we have suggested ways in which you might demonstrate your credentials and address the concerns.

1. Qualifications

- Chartered firm/IFP Accredited designation.
- All advisers QCA level 4 and Gap Filled.
- All advisers hold their personal Statement of Professional Standing.
- Case studies showcasing your best work.
- Genuine testimonials from delighted clients.

2. Advice driven not Sales driven model

- Copy of your documented service proposition, your promise to your clients.
- Testimonials.
- Existing successful referral relationships, but be discreet.

3. Willing to build a relationship

- Clearly defined "Professional Partners Service Standards".
- Regular structured training for partners and fee earners.
- Regular "Relationship Review" meetings.
- Robust communication framework to keep partners informed.
- Structured, professional engagement process.
- Supply relevant and interesting content for their client communications.

4. Minimising reputational risk

- Testimonials.
- Case Studies.
- Direct client feedback post advice process.
- Existing strong reputation.
- Copies of all reports and recommendations (subject to client agreement).
- Test Case using a partner or fee earner.

5. Clarity around what you do and how you do it

- Clear documented client propositions and communications materials, particularly your website.
- Ideal client profiles.
- High quality sample client reports.
- Site visit to your office to meet key people and see elements of your process.

6. Ability to cross refer

- Explain that your advice can enhance and deepen their existing client relationships.
- Show them examples of how working with you may lead to more fee work for them, (e.g. trusts, wills, powers of attorney, property protection trusts).
- Give all your professional partners an undertaking that you will not disturb existing client relationships of the partner firms you work with.
- This is no place for bull****. Manage their expectations and be realistic.

End of Stage 3: Initial Meeting Checklist

Here are your Actions for Implementation from stage 3

1. Develop a list of great questions to ask.

2. Create a slide deck for your first meeting presentation.

3. Develop a range of Professional Partner Service Standards that are appropriate for your business.

4. Conduct an honest appraisal of how you stack up against the common selection criteria and establish how you will evidence your credentials in each area.

07

Stage 4: Nurture

"Nurturing" might be the 4th stage in the relationship development process, but remember, we have only just completed the first meeting, so it is still very early days.

Your objectives have to reflect that.

I was speaking recently to the owner of a business that arranges appointments for advisers with accountants and solicitors. He told me about one adviser for whom they had arranged an appointment with a local solicitor.

As part of their "appointment quality audit" they always speak to both the adviser and the solicitor or accountant after each meeting. The feedback from the adviser was that the meeting didn't go at all well and the chances of the firm referring clients was practically non-existent.

So he phoned the solicitor to get their version of events. The feedback from her was that the meeting had gone really well. She had been really impressed with what the adviser had said, but she just wasn't prepared to sign an introducer agreement at the very first meeting.

That example illustrates perfectly what we've been saying from the outset. You have to take the relationship through the know, like, trust stage before other professionals will let you within a million miles of their clients. Pulling a pre-prepared introducer agreement out of your briefcase during the first meeting is completely inappropriate. The sad thing is that it sounds like the adviser had really done everything right up until that point.

Objectives

I believe that the key things you should be trying to achieve in the nurturing stage are:

- To continue to establish your credibility, by building on the great work you did during the first meeting.
- To demonstrate that you understand the issues and challenges they are facing by talking more about the impact those challenges are having on them and their practice.
- To differentiate your approach from other approaches they may have had in the past and crucially,
- To gain commitment to proceed to the next stage which this time is actually to reach an agreement in principle to refer a test case.

Key activities and actions

So what are the key actions and activities required during this stage. Well, as we've said, the nurturing stage starts after the initial meeting, once your target firm seem genuinely interested and serious about continuing the dialogue and maintaining momentum.

The key set piece event at this stage should be to try to get your message across to all the partners and key decision makers within the practice by arranging a more detailed follow-up presentation.

The need for this will depend on the size of the firm. In a small single practitioner firm, it might simply be a case of going into more detail about the specific referral opportunities and looking at one or two case studies and perhaps some testimonials, just to offer tangible proof of happy clients. In a bigger firm this is likely to be a more formal event and key to getting to the next stage. The presentation itself will have to cover off all the things that the first meeting presentation does but widen out into other areas. In particular, it's going to be content that includes:

- Reaffirming their strategic goals objectives and challenges to show you actually listened.
- An "about us" section to provide hard evidence about how you satisfy the 6 key selection criteria that we looked at in the previous chapter.
- What makes your business different – why should they choose to work with you rather than any other firm that might approach them? What is it that sets you apart? This may need to include more detail than you did in the initial meeting presentation.
- A case study or two, to showcase your best work and maybe a handful of compelling genuine client testimonials to provide the all-important social proof that you actually deliver what you say.

- An outline of some of the main financial planning synergies and opportunities, ideally relating to their specific areas of specialism as a firm.

You might also offer to use one of the partners or fee earners themselves, as a "guinea pig" or test case so that they can experience first hand the quality of your advice, service and process. It's totally up to you how, or even whether, you charge for doing this, but it can be a really effective way to "walk the talk" and provide clear practical evidence and experience of your advice process in action.

Either way, I would certainly raise the issue of a test case early in the relationship, whether it be one of their clients, or an individual within the firm itself. It shows real intent on your part and can be an indicator of buy-in on theirs. Without the test case, you can't show them the impact of what you do.

Assuming the meeting goes well and they still seem keen to develop the relationship further it's then time to deploy a range of "nurturing strategies" and find reasons and excuses to keep in touch, to maintain the momentum that all your work to this point has generated.

This is often where relationships wither. The lack of a clearly defined contact strategy often results in a loss of focus and momentum for you and a loss of interest for them. Let's take a look at some potential tactics.

Nurturing strategies and tactics

The first caveat is that you really need to be pretty confident that the firm in question is serious about developing a two way relationship before you start to invest the time and energy needed to execute some of the things we are going to talk about.

In fact the nurturing stage and the formal implementation stage shouldn't be a long engagement, you want to always be moving towards a formal referral relationship, so managing the time line here is critical.

1. Lunch and learn seminars

These are a great way to demonstrate your expertise and establish credibility. They are also a tangible demonstration of your willingness to spend time on developing the relationship.

The objectives of lunch and learn sessions are...

- To demonstrate the range, breadth and depth of your expertise.
- To connect each topic with an obvious and immediate area of interest to the partners and fee earners.
- To develop the range of referrals and increase the number of partners and fee earners referring.

Essentially, lunch and learn events are training and education sessions to identify where the financial planning and referral opportunities lie, and how they relate to specific accountancy or legal specialisms.

I'd also suggest that you supply the lunch, at least for the first one!

These events are a great opportunity to demonstrate the many ways in which you can work together to deliver even better overall outcomes for clients and offer a co-ordinated, joined up, comprehensive service. It is also the most effective and tangible demonstration of your genuine commitment to the relationship.

2. Business development meetings

Group and individual business development meetings with partners and fee earners help to keep referrals front of mind. If you just sit back and wait for the referrals to come, you're unlikely to get the results you want.

The objectives of business development meetings are;

- To encourage a proactive approach to looking for introductions to clients and of course, identifying further accounting or legal needs that such clients might have in order to create additional revenue for the firm itself.
- To work with them to identify clients who fall into areas of advice most likely to offer the best opportunities to make a real difference.
- To discuss joint seminars for specific client groups, target markets or areas of advice.

- To develop and maintain a consistent, sustained and regular flow of high quality client referrals. You might, for example have short, but regular meetings with individual partners and fee earners to discuss current and past clients and encourage a regular flow of referrals.

Ideas for staying "front of mind"

Particularly in the early days, it's important to be in regular contact with each partner and fee earner. Finding legitimate reasons to communicate and maintain contact so that you can continue to build trust and credibility and to build a personal relationship and professional image with as many of the team as possible.

Here are some simple quick and highly effective ways you can do so.

- Supply content for their client newsletter or a blog on their website.
- Keep in touch through regular calls/emails.
- Regular communications about client work in progress.
- Send an e-newsletter to, or run regular webinars for, all your professional connections.
- Send specific emails on key issues / legislative changes.
- Organise social events or provide occasional hospitality.

- Run quarterly seminars on relevant topics of mutual interest.

I appreciate that some of these ideas assume that you've already got your business in great shape and you've got the capacity to do all these things.

The first observation I'd make is that you don't have to do all the things I've suggested. They are just some of the ways that you can keep your name and brand at the front of their thinking, because this stage of the process is where things can and do stagnate due to a lack of creative ideas about how to keep in touch. If you are not actively managing the relationship, they will simply get back on their hamster wheel and forget to proactively look for referral opportunities. You simply have to take responsibility for maintaining progress and momentum.

Another concern many advisers express is the cost involved. These services aren't expensive. Maybe a modest set up cost of £100 or so and a regular monthly fee of £15 for a newsletter, £25 per month for something like "Go to Meeting" or "Webex" to host your webinar programme. In the context of the reach these tools provide, the costs really are insignificant. Yes they all take time, but building any new relationship, personal or business, requires you to invest some time if you want it to work.

08

Stage 5: Implementation

You'll remember that we said in the previous chapter, that the implementation and nurturing stages should be almost concurrent, to avoid putting in masses of work without some clear buying signals from the firms you have been targeting.

So the key activities of the implementation stage cut across both the nurturing and implementation stages.

It's also fair to say that if you have nurtured the relationship effectively to this point, "Implementation" should be a doddle, as you've done most of the hard work.

The objectives of the implementation stage are:

- To really impress them, by reviewing and providing feedback on the test case. If you have used one of the partners or fee earners, this should be relatively straightforward. If you have worked with a real client, you will need to find a way to get specific feedback on the client's experience and feelings about the whole process, back to the firm in question.
- To reach an "in principle" agreement to establish a formal referral relationship.

The importance of the test case

The test case really is the "watershed moment". Without it you can't showcase your service. The lack of one can also be an indicator that there is no real buy-in on their part.

Remember, reputational damage is one of the key concerns solicitors and accountants have about referring their clients. Whilst by this point you will have reduced their concerns significantly, finding a way to get client feedback directly to the introducer can be a great way to reassure them that you are confident their clients will be delighted. And of course, the feedback will prove it!

Without some feedback from a test case client, they have nothing to judge your service against. Without it, implementation is a forlorn hope.

End of Stage 5: Implementation Checklist

Here are the critical things that you will need to do to implement the referral relationship effectively. Once again, these are structured in such a way that demonstrates a clear willingness to invest time in developing the relationship, but without over-committing you in terms of time and effort.

1. Organise (and maybe even deliver) the first monthly/quarterly training presentation (lunch and learn session) to partners and fee earners at their offices on the financial planning opportunities associated with a specific specialism. The presentation should cover:

   - Where the specific opportunities are.
   - Ideal client profiles of the types of client that the issue in question will be relevant to (what do they look like, what words or phrases might give them away as an ideal candidate for advice).
   - Case studies to showcase the impact that your advice is likely to have on the client.
   - Getting feedback from the fee earners after each presentation to check understanding and answer questions and concerns. Maybe follow up with them to identify specific clients who might benefit from advice right now.

2. Organise or invite them to visit your office (again dependent on the size of your firm) to:

- Meet the team.
- Walk them through your client engagement/advice processes.
- Demonstrate key planning systems.
- Show sample reports.

Put together a professional, well planned and co-ordinated event to effectively seal the deal. If this goes well, the implementation decision will be easy.

3. Subscribe all partners and fee earners to your client and "Professional Partners" newsletter.

4. Offer to write relevant content to be included in their client communications.

5. Prepare your ongoing contact plan, so your nurturing tactics continue in a structured way to make sure that the relationship stays strong and that you stay front of mind.

09

Stage 6:
Build & Embed

So, if you've moved the relationship this far forward, you are well and truly in the home straight. Let's look at the specific objectives for this final phase, because having put in this much work it would be a travesty to fall at the last hurdle wouldn't it?

The objectives of the Build and Embed stage are simple:

- To formalise the relationship.
- To generate a consistent and sustainable flow of ideal client referrals and to increase that over time as the relationship develops.
- To lock out your competitors.

Joint marketing plans

Creating a joint marketing plan is a great way to generate real intent and momentum. By working together to identify what objectives you want to achieve from the relationship, which types of client you will be focusing on and how you intend to go about reaching them, you can establish real enthusiasm and momentum.

In fact, in a large firm, particularly a legal practice, it might be an idea to develop a marketing plan at the departmental level to make sure that you can focus on specific client types and client problems, rather than trying to create a plan that tries to cover every eventual client scenario.

Be specific about each target audience and try to identify the high level strategies and tactics you'll use to find them. For example, it might be through identifying existing dormant clients with relevant needs. It might be through seminars, it might be through writing to specific client niches about relevant topics.

Then capture the specific actions that will be required each month to execute the plan. Make sure each action has an owner and a deadline and of course, wherever possible, you'll need to take as much leg work as you can out of the process for the firm itself.

Measuring results

Establishing a Management Information dashboard is essential to help you measure the success of the relationship. Keep it simple by just capturing the client name, the name of the referring partner or fee earner, date of referral, date the client was contacted, potential revenue or fee and a field to record the current status of each referral (in other words, where the client is in the advice process).

Of course, you might want to add additional fields to measure other things. For example, in a larger firm it might make sense to record, the revenue generated by each partner and fee earner. You will need to be careful how, or even whether, you share this information publicly, but it will give you a great insight into who's referring and who isn't.

It would certainly be a document I'd want to use with the managing or senior partner as part of the regular relationship review meetings.

End of Stage 6: Build and Embed checklist

So what are the key actions and activities of the build and embed stage? By this time you will know your audience pretty well and will be able to tailor your approach accordingly. Here are some specific activities I'd recommend, though of course, you might not feel able to commit to doing all of these, but some of them should certainly be very much on your radar, or you could undo all the hard work to this point.

Each of these actions can be classified as Social, Operational or Measurement.

Social

1. Keep in touch informally with the managing/senior partner with the occasional phone call or email.

2. Maybe organise a celebratory launch reception with drinks and canapes at your (or their) office to celebrate the fact that there has been an agreement to work together.

3. Celebrate successes from time to time, through social events and personalised thank you cards. You might also want to offer incentives to encourage referrals either on an individual or team basis or even set up little internal competitions between departments with modest prizes for those who refer the most or highest value referrals.

Operational

1. Arrange the first "Relationship Review" meeting with the managing partner or key contact. In the early days in particular, it's important to check in with them on a regular basis and to make sure that the relationship is working for all parties... for them, for their clients and of course, for you. These meetings will give you both an opportunity to raise and discuss any concerns you have. For you that may be the rate of referrals being received or maybe even about specific partners/fee earners or departments who seem less proactive about making referrals.

2. I think it makes sense to schedule these relationship review meetings monthly for the first 3 – 6 months. If the frequency is any less than that, you won't get a chance, for example, to raise any concerns you have if referrals don't materialise.

3. Call each fee earner to ensure they are "onboard" and have everything they need.

4. Implement the ongoing contact plan. Continue with the nurturing strategies we outlined at Stage 4.

5. Develop a library of appropriate presentations and other content for the lunch and learn sessions, for potential joint seminars and for their regular client communications.

6. Explore and establish regular joint marketing initiatives and client events.

Measurement

1. Create a Management Information dashboard to measure success. This is important from your perspective to measure the return on the investment of time you've made. You might also want to share (and I'd recommend you do) some parts of the MI dashboard with them. If they are genuinely bought in, they too will be interested to see how it's working.

2. And if the relationship really works well you might want to formalise it by, for example, establishing a JV if appropriate, but it makes sense to live together successfully for a while, before deciding to get married as it were.

10

What next?

I really do appreciate you taking the time to read "Professional Partners Success Blueprint". I hope you have enjoyed reading it as much as I enjoyed writing it. More importantly I hope you have found the step by step framework helpful.

Most of all I hope it inspires you to take action. To use everything we've talked about and to get a return on the investment of time that you made to read the book.

Managing your expectations

At this point it is worth outlining my thoughts on the timeframe over which each of these six stages of the relationship development process is likely to occur. There are no hard and fast rules. We've seen IFA clients who have started to receive a steady flow of referrals after just a couple of meetings. However, that isn't typical.

I know of high profile firms who have invested more than 5 years in developing relationships that work. There are no magic bullets. Nobody said it was easy.

Remember we identified that expecting results too soon and giving up too quickly were amongst the most common mistakes advisers make when executing their professional partners strategy.

I would urge you to see the process as a two year project, where year 1 is about building the foundations, through stages 1 to 5, and year 2 is all about building and embedding the relationships.

You will have some wins along the way and should get a reasonable number of referrals in the first year if you follow the framework outlined in this book in a consistent and structured way. But you have to commit to this as a long term strategy.

I'd love to hear your success stories (and your disasters) and the results you actually achieve.

Please do drop me an email to steve@stevebillingham.com with your stories.

I'd also love to hear what you thought of the book. Which elements did you find the most helpful?

Experience tells me that if you haven't taken what you've learned in these pages and done something with it in the next 28 days, you probably never will. And that would be such a shame. This "stuff" works. We've got clients who have followed this framework and seen instant success.

Having taken you step by step through the things you need to do, I'll leave you with four specific final pieces of advice about what NOT to do. Four golden rules that shouldn't be broken.

- Don't lecture about the challenges they face – simply engage them in conversation.

- Don't persist with those who aren't interested or are unresponsive to your calls and emails.
- Don't refer to "products" or "commission" in your meetings… EVER!
- Don't spread yourself too thinly – take things slowly and see which relationships develop.

I wrote this book to help advisers finally make the breakthrough they've been striving for. I'd love you to be one of them.

If you think you need more hands-on help and tailored input in formulating and executing your professional partners strategy, please email me and we can schedule an initial conversation about what you need and how I can help.

I wish each of you the best of luck in developing your own strategy and creating a sustainable and predictable flow of high quality referrals.

11

How to network effectively

by Carrie Bendall

Love it or hate it, if you are going to grow your business, you must invest in networking to succeed. It's one of the most effective and cost effective tools at your disposal, tried and tested for centuries if not millennia.

By networking, I mean face-to-face and human. I see it as the act of expanding your personal network of contacts with the aim of attracting more of the right kind of clients to your business either directly or indirectly through professional connections. You can't sit at your desk behind your technology and expect these contacts to magically appear. You have to dedicate energy and time to going out and finding them.

Any scepticism you may have may be rooted in a dread of doing it or some poor past experience.

Just Google 'networking' or 'business networking' and explore it a bit. One of the news items you may find is the appointment of Julia Hobsbawm as the first professor in business networking at London's Cass Business School and now at University College Suffolk in Bury St Edmunds. Julia is also founder of Editorial Intelligence, a highly acclaimed and globally recognised knowledge networking business. Julia believes that as we have come to accept Chief Information Officers and Chief Technology Officers, we will soon be seeing Chief Networking Officers.

Take our author Steve Billingham. From a standing start on day one when he set up his consulting business in 2010, he is now incredibly successful, limiting the number of clients he can take on. The word "incredibly" might suggest an element of surprise. Not at all. Steve's success is down to the fact that he knows who to talk to and where to find them. He knows the best events and where to be seen speaking. He knows what to write and where to write, and he knows how important it is to deliver time and time again, consistently. What is incredible is the passion, doing and delivery power.

Fundamentally networking is about being clear about what you want to achieve and then getting out there to meet people who will help you do it. But it needs to be done with the right spirit. Forget lead generation and the desire to collect as many business cards as possible. This is about quality, not quantity. It's about generosity and the desire to make some new friends who may well be able to help you grow your business.

You need a plan

As you will have read throughout the pages of this book, preparation is key. Just as you need a business plan, you need to have a plan for networking to give you focus.

This preparation involves:

1. Setting your house in order

- Being happy about your purpose.
- Tweaking your '60 seconds' so that you can imagine it as a conversation rather than a 60 second spurt. Focusing on the personal you, the people are going to be more interested in you the individual rather than your job spec. If you don't have a passion (apart from your business) find one. Wine tasting, golf, running, local theatre.
- Being confident about your identity, your website, your LinkedIn profile, your business card.
- Think about what you might wear. First impressions are important, but it is as important to be yourself.

2. Targeting who you want to meet

- Know who you are looking for.
- Think of your favourite and best clients.
- Where are you going to find more of them? Which clubs do they belong to?
- Think about your existing network. Your family, friends, previous and current colleagues, your professional connections and your own clubs.

3. Researching online

- Discover what's happening in your area.

- Look at accountant and solicitor websites to see what events they are putting on.
- Look at business networks such as the Institute of Directors in your local area, your local chamber of commerce.
- Look at what you enjoy doing and see if you can combine the two. Our local IoD has just organised a wine tasting evening.
- It's always a good idea to stick with something that interests you in the first place.
- Think a bit more laterally, where are the people you want to meet going to be.

4. Mapping out your plan

- How much time are you going to dedicate to this?
- A day a week?
- How many events can you attend in a month?
- Month after month?
- Include a way of measuring success.

5. Think about your first conversation

- Not about your mini one-way advert for your business but of things that are interesting you at the moment.
- Just your name is a good starting point. That normally gets a name back and another question that you can answer and the conversation has started.

Attending events

For most, arriving at an event where you expect to know no one is an excruciatingly painful prospect. If this is the case for you, you will be in good company. There are two approaches. Pick an event where you will find people you know or, take someone with you who you can feed off, introducing each other and encouraging other people to join your conversation.

Give yourself plenty of time to get there so that you are not rushing. Take time to look around and enter the room. You have as much right to be there as anyone else so walk in with confidence and help others who may be hanging back.

Firm handshakes, eye contact and open body language. Always stand so that you can be approached easily, even if you are in deep conversation, although the person you are with needs to have your attention and politeness if you want to move on.

The most important qualities to bring to the fore are your listening and questioning skills. You need to be curious about the people you are talking to, interested and then interesting. Try to hold back your opinions, let others speak and do all the hard work for you.

If you can offer help, do.

Remember, your sole purpose is to make new friends, gathering and sharing information as you go. Be generous. Give first.

Follow up

Make sure you do what you say you will. If you've made any promises, act on them as soon as you can.

Find a way of remembering names, particularly of the people you liked. Think about ways you can meet again.

As you know from your own client relationships it takes a while for the know, like, trust pattern to emerge.

Keep at it

You have to have quite a tough skin. Don't be put off if initial contact and conversations don't work. You can't get on with everyone.

Networking is a long-term activity and a slow burn. It's a time to be personal and personable, to be curious about others and to be interesting. You need to set yourself apart by being the person that everyone wants to know.

About the Author

Steve has worked in the financial services sector since 1984.

Throughout that time he has worked alongside financial advisers and planners, accountants and solicitors in sales, senior management and consultancy positions.

He was a member of the senior management team of one of the UK's leading life assurance, investment and pension providers for over 20 years, leading key strategic and operational change programmes and spearheading adviser engagement and education activity in respect of the impact of regulatory change on client relationships.

Since 2008, Steve has worked with financial planning and advisory businesses of all shapes and sizes, providing strategic, operational and marketing consultancy and implementation support, to help them grow their business, increase revenues and improve profitability.

He is known for his practical, action-orientated approach and his ability to help advisers rediscover their passion and enthusiasm for what they do. Clients value his straight talking (a throwback to his Yorkshire roots) and his reliable, passionate and responsive attitude towards their business. They also appreciate the "external accountability" that he brings, which helps them to make real tangible progress on their key actions and priorities.

Steve writes regularly in the media and is a frequent and sought after speaker at industry events. He provides practical practice management insights through his blog at www.stevebillingham.com/blog and his monthly "Business Insights" newsletter.

Steve now lives in Sussex, with his wife Sue, but still hasn't lost his "northern grit" or the Yorkshire accent!

Printed in Germany
by Amazon Distribution
GmbH, Leipzig

Printed in Germany
by Amazon Distribution
GmbH, Leipzig